STILL IN THE FAMILY TREE

GROWING UP IN KINSHIP CARE WITH EXTENDED FAMILY OR FRIENDS

HOLLY MARLOW

ISBN for paperback: 978-1-0685230-1-4

DEDICATION

For my parents, who showed me that family steps up.

ACKNOWLEDGEMENTS

Endless thanks to my wonderful husband Jon, who has supported me in more ways than I could ever list. Love you and our amazing children always.

Thank you to my spectacular sister, Suzy Garland, for creating the original Caring Goose character featured in this story and in *Delly Duck: Why A Little Chick Couldn't Stay With His Birth Mother*, *Room in the Nest: A Foster Care Story*, *The Adoption Ceremony* and *Some Things Have Changed*.

Thank you to my brilliant son, Jake, who at 5 years old drew the excellent picture that the magpie chick on this page is working on, and asked me to include it in this book!

High in the branches of their family tree, two young magpies played in their nest. Rowan and Ash lived with their parents, Drift and Flinch, but life in the nest sometimes felt a bit wobbly. Rowan and Ash didn't always know what to expect.

Some days, Drift and Flinch brought Rowan and Ash lots of worms for breakfast, but some days, they didn't bring home anything to eat.

Sometimes, Drift and Flinch flew off and left the chicks in the nest for a long time. Rowan and Ash felt cold, hungry and scared when Drift and Flinch went away.

Some nights, Drift and Flinch argued loudly. This upset the magpie chicks, and they couldn't sleep.

A little bird told Caring Goose that the magpie chicks weren't being looked after properly, so Caring Goose visited the family tree to see if she could help the magpie family. She saw that Rowan and Ash needed more care and attention.

Caring Goose explained to Drift and Flinch that it is important to keep chicks safe and warm, and to give them enough healthy food. Over the next few weeks, Caring Goose kept coming back to check on the magpie family. She tried to help Drift and Flinch to look after Rowan and Ash properly.

Unfortunately, even with Caring Goose's help, things didn't get much better. Drift and Flinch kept leaving Rowan and Ash in the nest for a long time, and they kept forgetting to feed them.

Caring Goose noticed some other magpies in the family tree, who loved Rowan and Ash, and knew how to keep chicks safe. Their names were Moss and Ember, and they were kind and gentle.

Caring Goose went to see the Wise Owl, who knew a lot about keeping little birds safe, and could make important decisions about families. Caring Goose told her all her worries about the magpie chicks not being looked after properly.

The Wise Owl listened and thought, then she asked Caring Goose to bring Drift and Flinch to see her. The Wise Owl asked Drift and Flinch about their lives, and about Rowan and Ash. She listened carefully to everything they had to say.

Then the Wise Owl spoke to Moss and Ember, and asked them what they knew about looking after chicks, and keeping them safe. After the Wise Owl had listened to everyone who knew and cared about the magpie family, she thought very carefully, then she made a big decision.

To make sure that Rowan and Ash would be safe and loved, they would live with Moss and Ember. Drift and Flinch could come to visit Rowan and Ash sometimes, but Moss and Ember would be in charge of looking after the magpie chicks from now on.

Moss and Ember's nest was a little higher up in the family tree than the magpie chicks were used to, but it felt soft and cosy. Sometimes Drift and Flinch came to visit Rowan and Ash, and they had a lovely time singing songs together.

Sometimes Drift and Flinch visited, but they seemed distracted and they didn't play properly. That made the chicks feel a bit frustrated. Sometimes they were late, or they didn't come. That made the chicks sad. They still didn't really know what to expect from Drift and Flinch.

But they knew what to expect from Moss and Ember. There were always tasty meals and lots of cuddles in Moss and Ember's nest. The magpie chicks felt safe and loved.

Rowan and Ash grew stronger and happier, and they got used to living on a different branch. They knew they could ask Moss and Ember any questions they had about Drift and Flinch, and they were happy that they still lived in the family tree.

Also by Holly Marlow

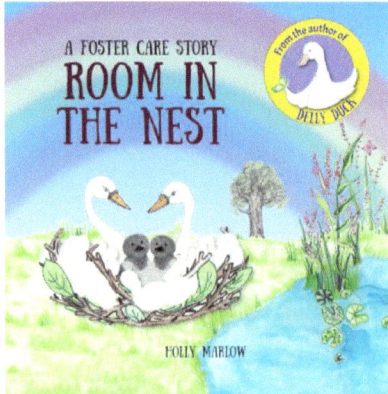

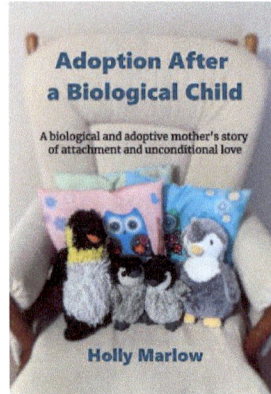

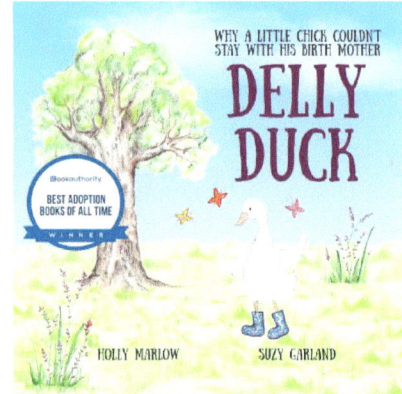

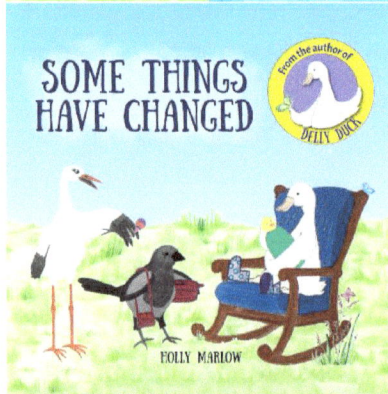

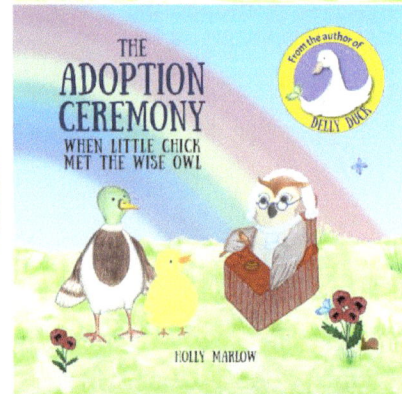

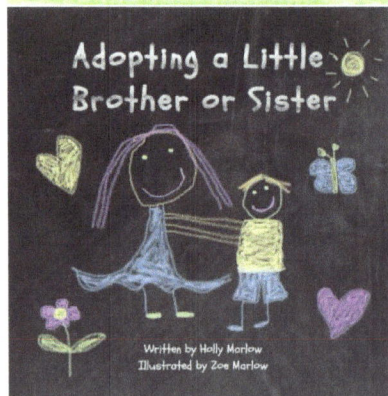

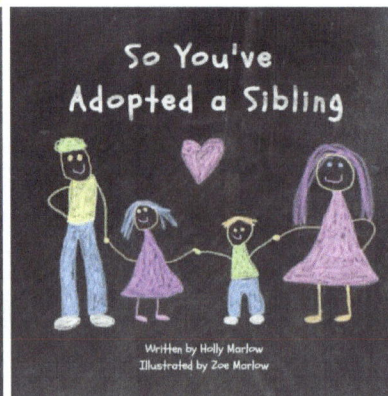

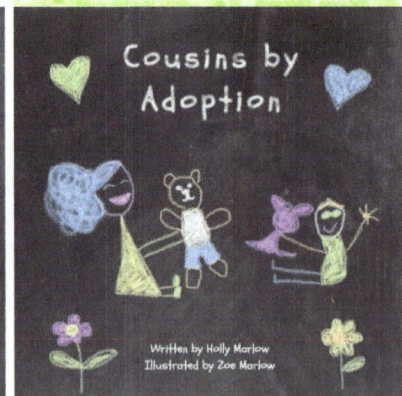

A FOSTER CARE STORY
ROOM IN THE NEST
from the author of DELLY DUCK
HOLLY MARLOW

Adoption After a Biological Child
A biological and adoptive mother's story of attachment and unconditional love
Holly Marlow

WHY A LITTLE CHICK COULDN'T STAY WITH HIS BIRTH MOTHER
DELLY DUCK
BEST ADOPTION BOOKS OF ALL TIME WINNER
HOLLY MARLOW   SUZY GARLAND

SOME THINGS HAVE CHANGED
from the author of DELLY DUCK
HOLLY MARLOW

THE **ADOPTION CEREMONY**
WHEN LITTLE CHICK MET THE WISE OWL
from the author of DELLY DUCK
HOLLY MARLOW

Adopting a Little Brother or Sister
Written by Holly Marlow
Illustrated by Zoe Marlow

So You've Adopted a Sibling
Written by Holly Marlow
Illustrated by Zoe Marlow

Cousins by Adoption
Written by Holly Marlow
Illustrated by Zoe Marlow

Please consider sharing your reviews on Amazon and social media!

Every family has their own story

Still in the Family Tree may be used to help children to understand how they have ended up living with special guardians or kinship carers, such as grandparents, aunts, uncles or family friends. Where there are differences in the life story of the child hearing the story, these can be reflected upon together. Some of the other books in this series may help support more in-depth discussions.

Many children will spend some time with a foster family, like Mr and Mrs Swan shown below, before moving to live with their kinship carers. If this fits with the story of the child you're reading this book to, you can simply show children the image below and explain that the magpies also lived with foster carers for a while, or *Room in the Nest* can be used to discuss foster care in more depth, and explore some of the possible outcomes from foster care that a judge may consider, including reunification with birth parents, family, adoption or long-term foster care.

Delly Duck uses metaphors to support deeper conversations about the reasons why a child may not be able to stay with their birth family. If a birth parent makes changes that mean a younger sibling is able to stay with them, *Some Things Have Changed* can be used to gently support discussion of the concerns that may be felt by an older child who is being raised in kinship care.

About the Author

Holly Marlow is an author and a parent to biological and adopted children. Holly strives for a gentle, therapeutic parenting style, and this has led her to create stories to help children to understand foster care, kinship care and adoption.

Holly enjoys travelling (especially searching for chameleons, geckos and snakes in the wild parts of Africa) and learning foreign languages. Holly has fibromyalgia and has spent a lot of time trying to raise awareness of the chronic pain condition, giving presentations in schools and universities. Holly enjoys baking and gardening, although she is terrible at both.

This story is illustrated by Holly, with some help from her younger sister, Suzy Garland, who drew the original Caring Goose character, and the beautiful family tree. Among her many talents and hobbies, Suzy is a wonderful mother and artist, and gardens far more successfully than her sister.

Visit **hollymarlow.com** for news on the latest and upcoming releases by this author, as well as webinars about life story work, a life story book template, and other resources to help explain adoption, foster care, kinship care and special guardianship.

www.ingramcontent.com/pod-product-compliance
Lightning Source LLC
LaVergne TN
LVHW072110070426
835509LV00002B/107